NOT FOR THE
FAINT OF HEART

Mazes Adults

ActivityCrusades

Published by Speedy Publishing Canada Limited

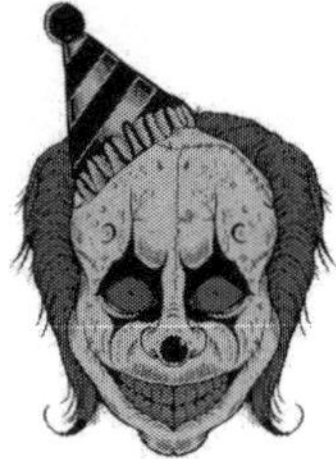

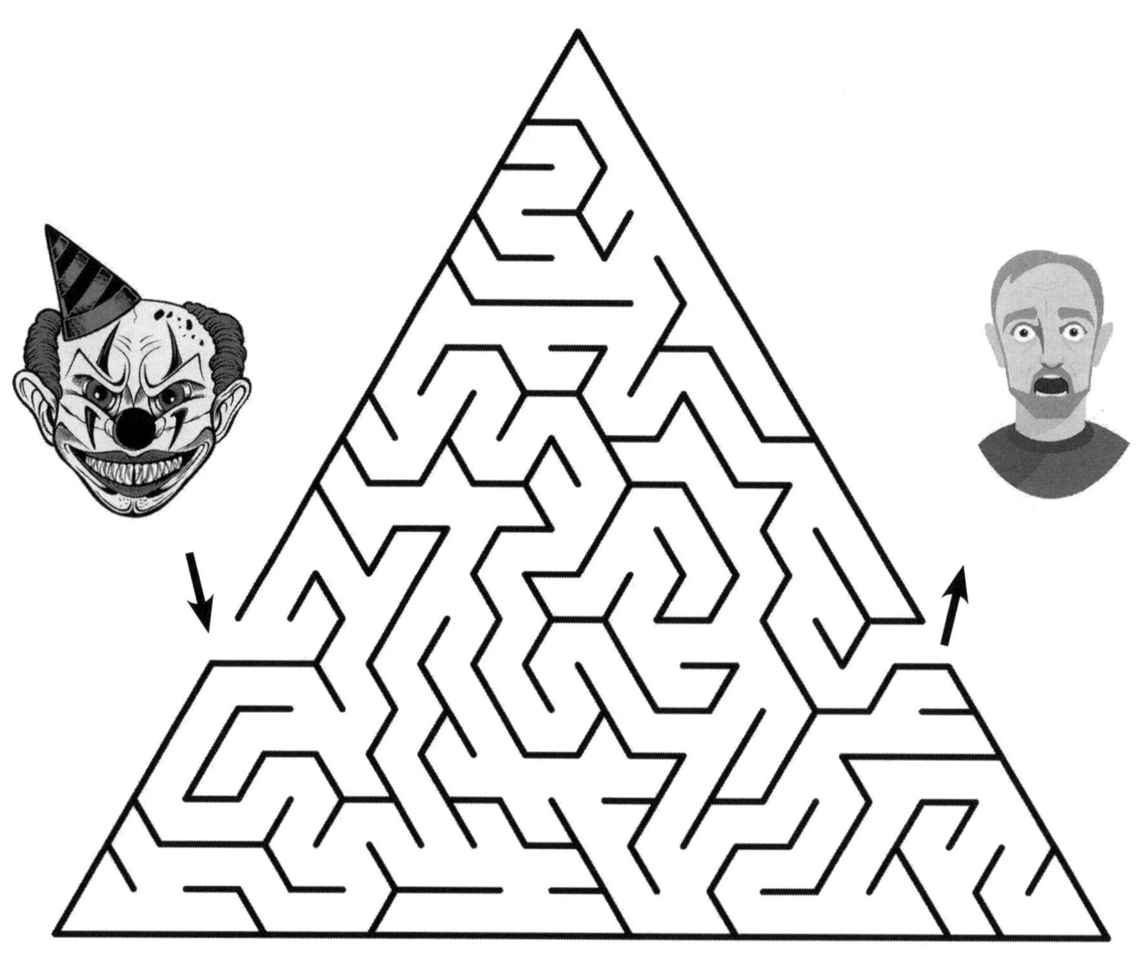

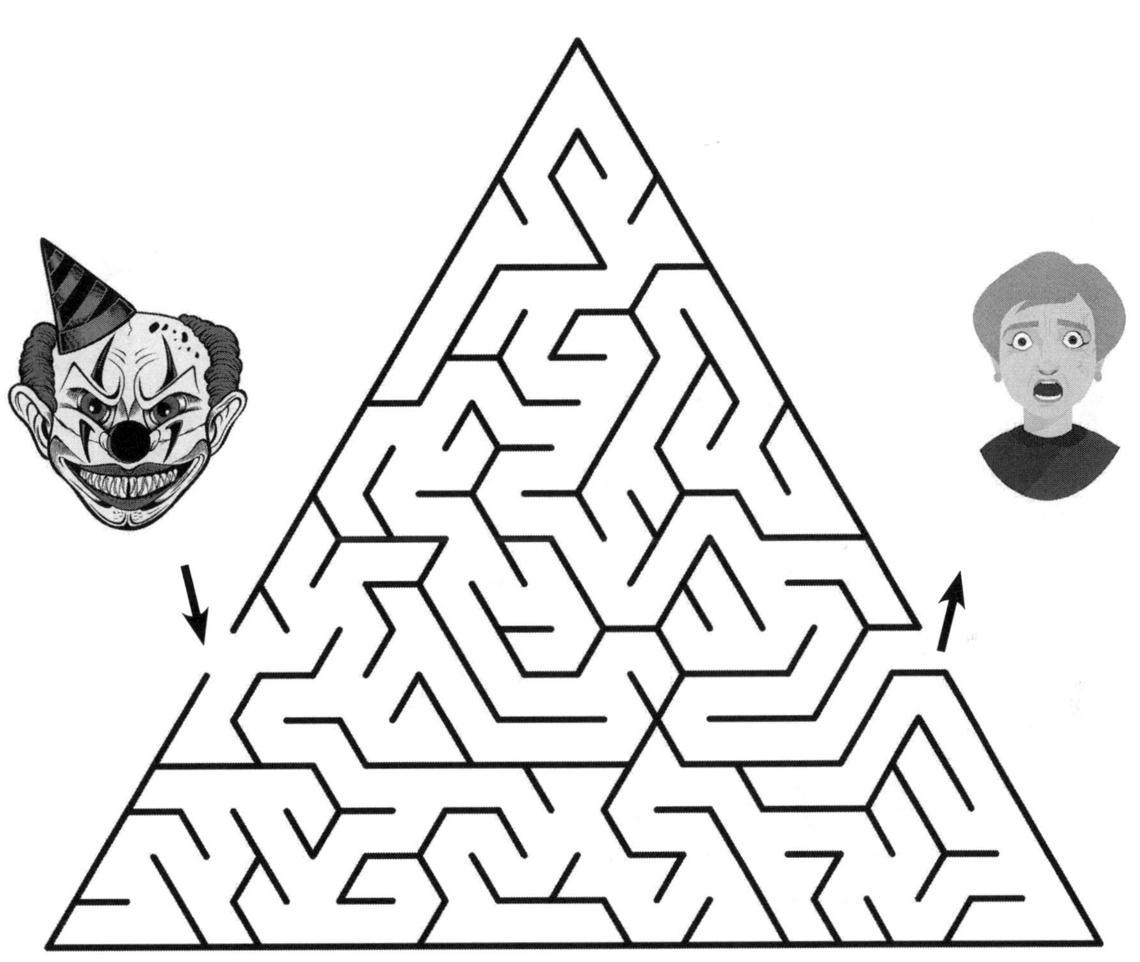

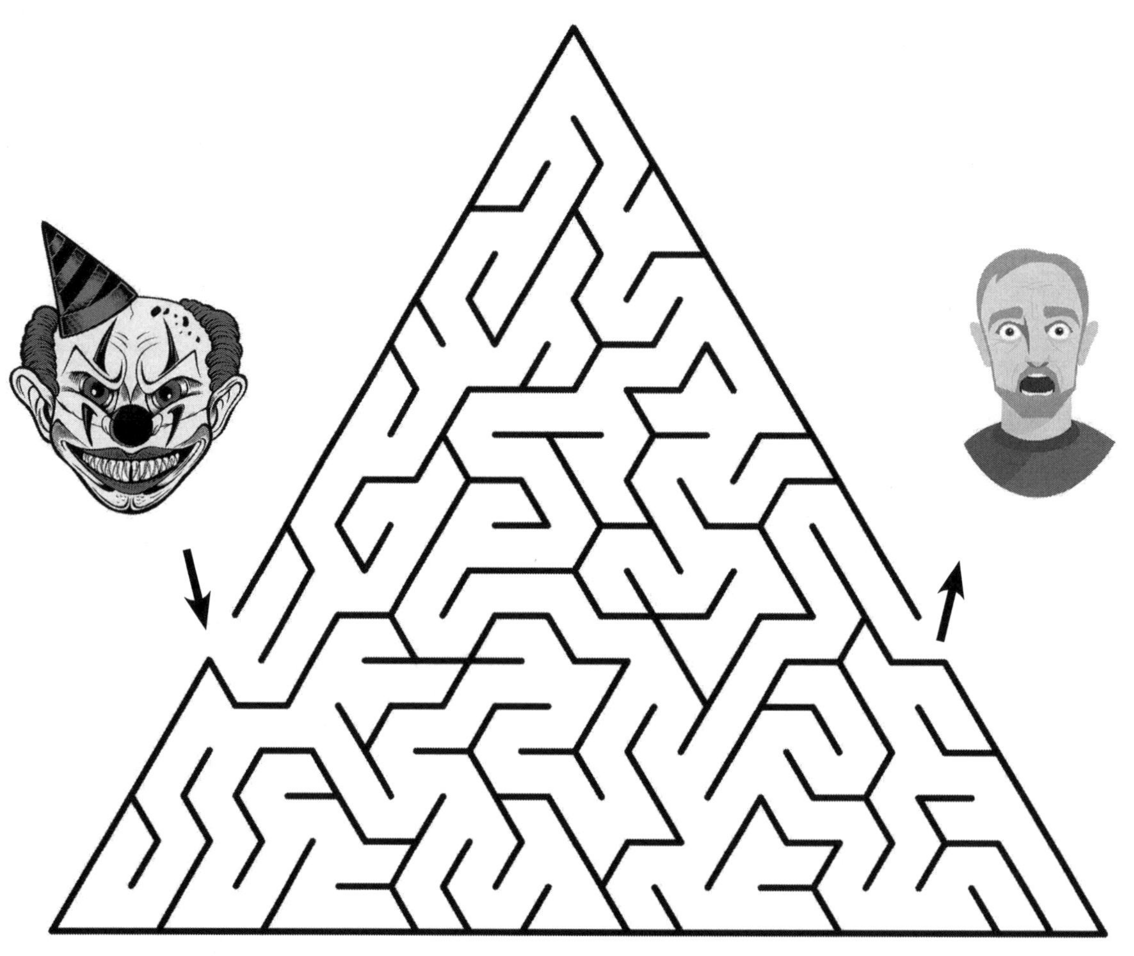

1

2

3

4

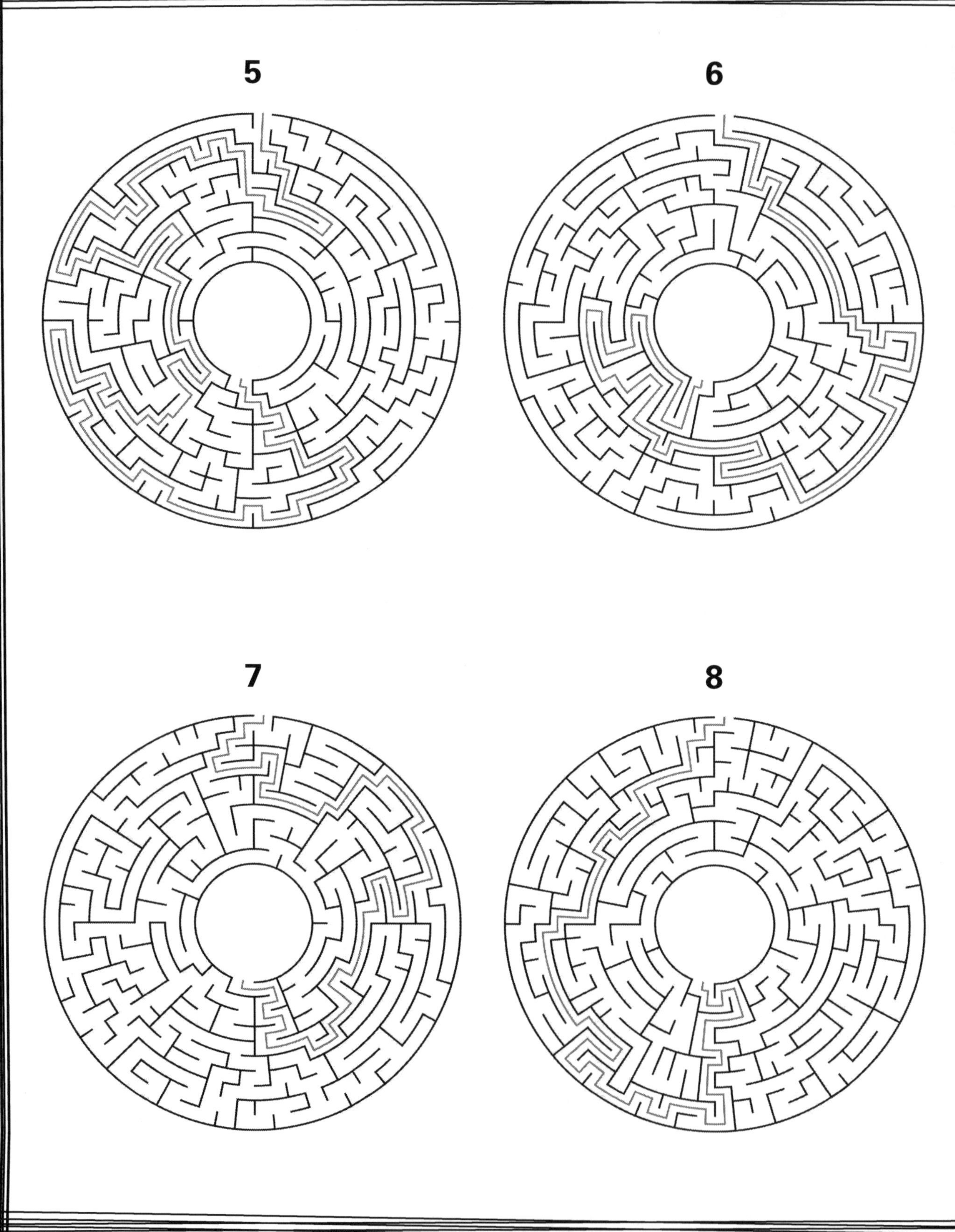

9

10

11

12

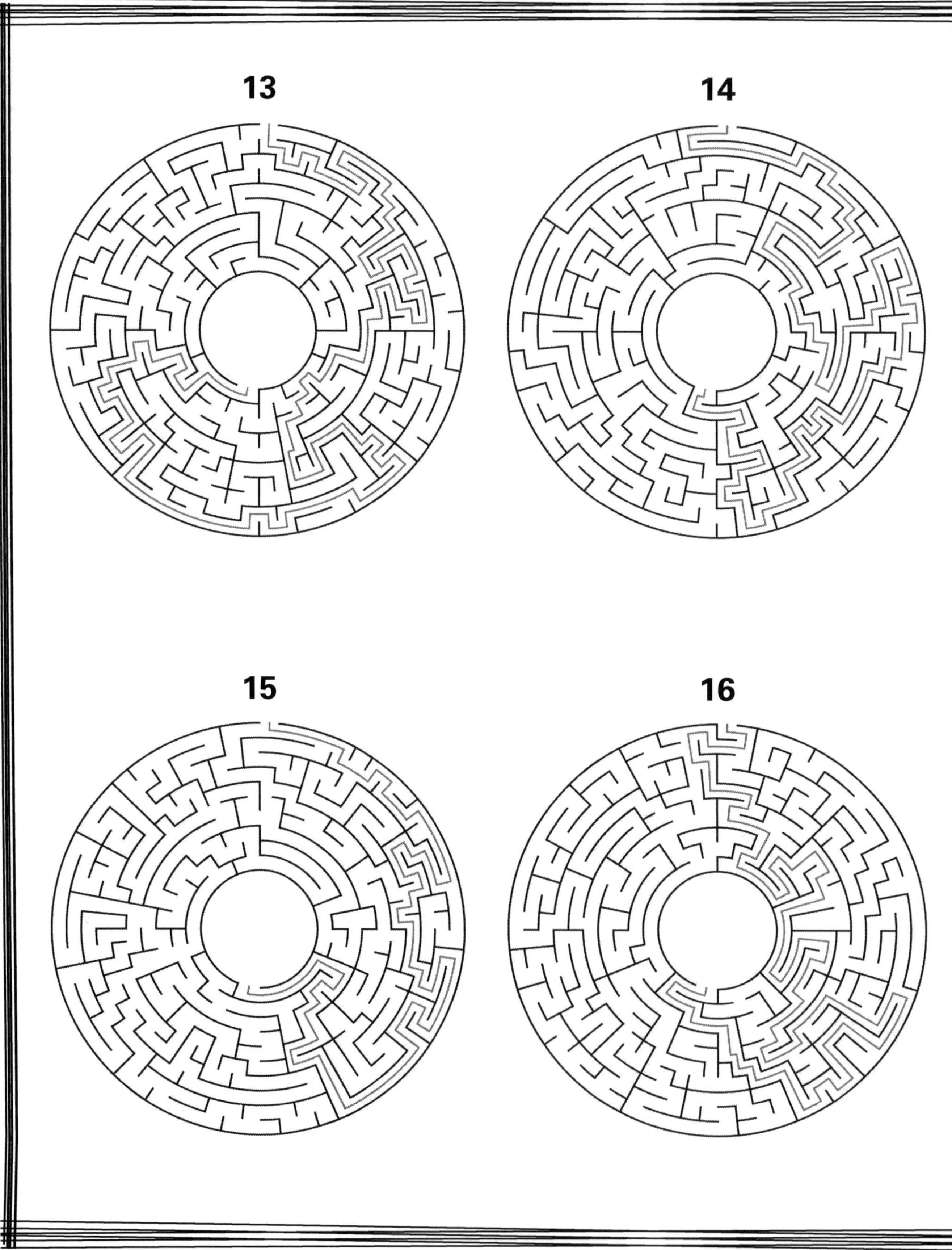

13

14

15

16

17

18

19

20

21

22

23

24

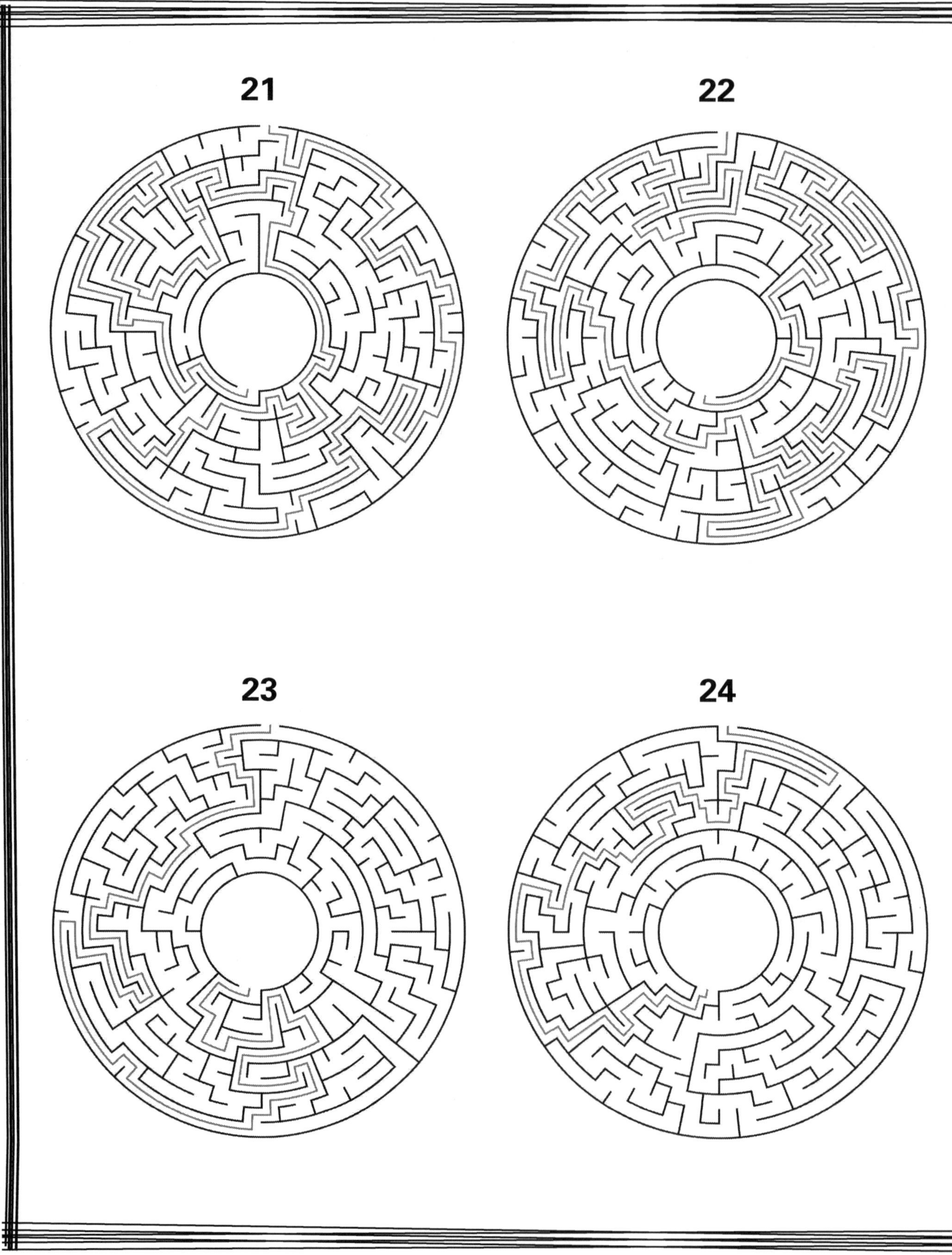

25

26

27

28

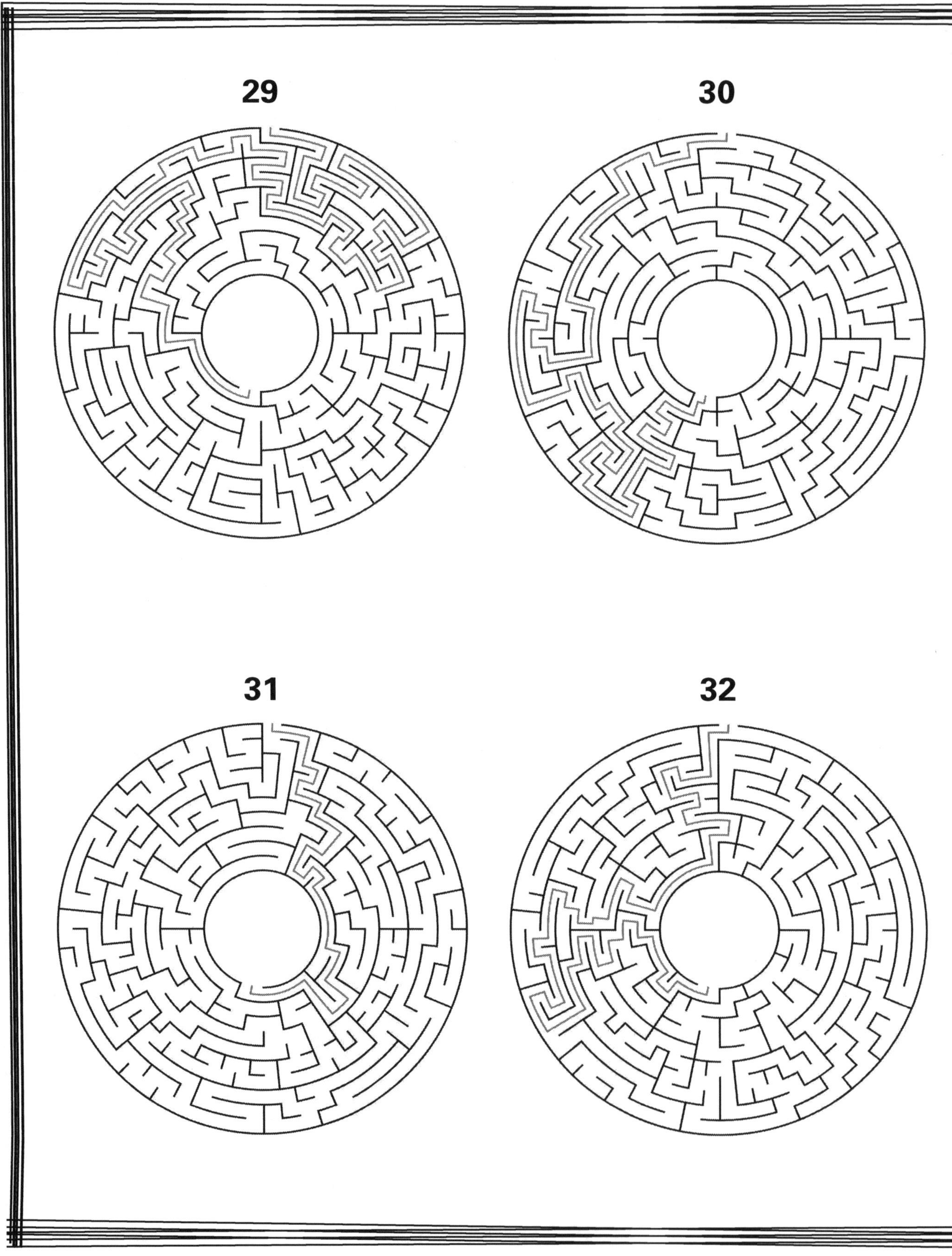

29
30
31
32

33

34

35

36

37
38
39
40

41

42

43

44

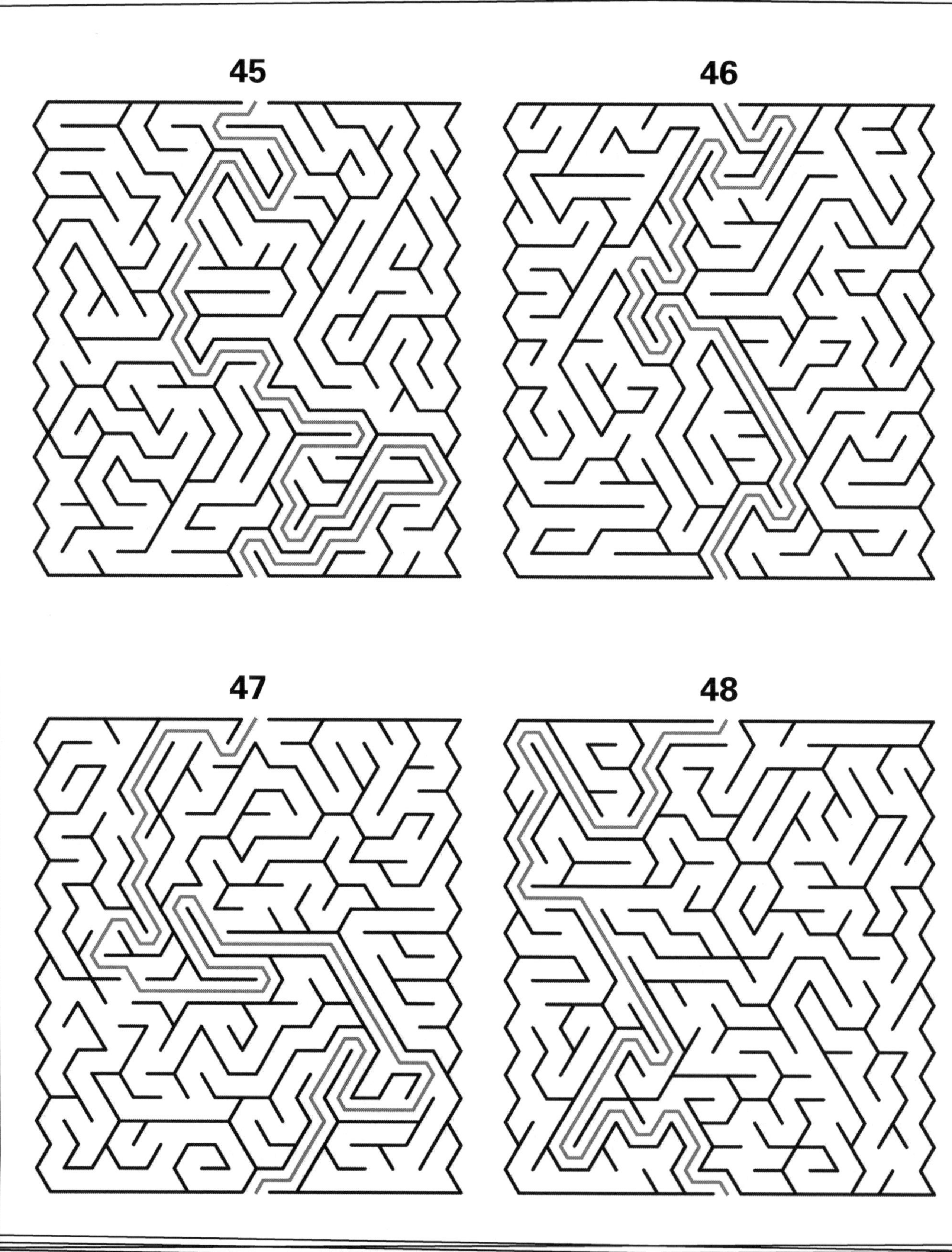

45
46
47
48

49

50

51

52

53

54

55

56

57

58

59

60

61

62

63

64

65

66

67

68

69

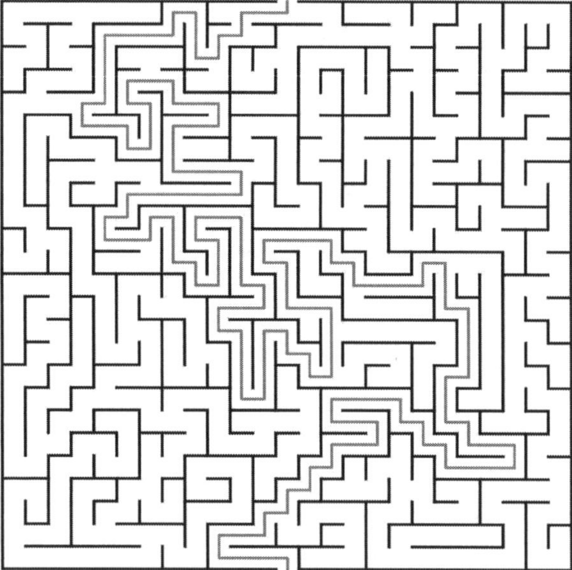

70

71

72

73

74

75

76

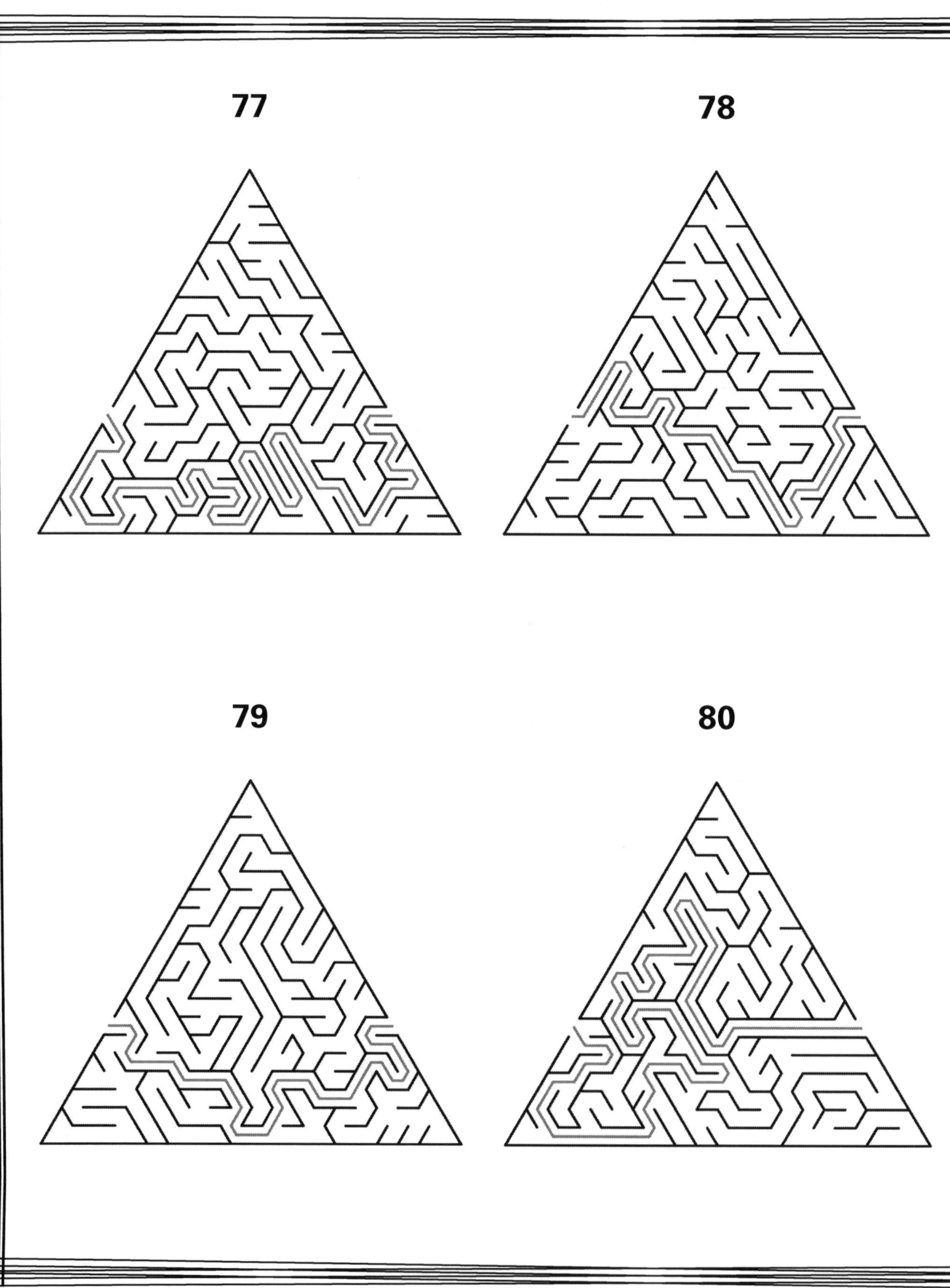

77
78
79
80

81

82